21 Ways to be a Kid Again & Get Adult Results

Praise for *21 Ways to be a Kid Again & Get Adult Results*

"As an Executive Coach, creativity and possibility thinking are always important to helping a client get from where they are to where they want to go. *21 Ways to be a Kid Again & Get Adult Results* bypasses the theoretical and leaps immediately into activities that guarantee the right brain neural pathways will be firing in new and wonderful ways. She reminds the reader of a simpler, more spontaneous time when creativity was just what we did all day long. The adult impact of reliving childhood play is to bring unfettered, unlimited thinking to any issue, problem, or opportunity adults encounter. Grab your hula hoop, Play-Doh and Legos, take off your shoes and go wading, and dance as if no one was watching, and I assure you no situation will be unsolvable!"

—David P. Mackinnon, Ph.D., M.B.A., President, Lighthouse Coaching LLC

"Kristen Eckstein takes us back to an era of candid innocence. 21 Ways to be a Kid Again & Get Adult Results reminds us that Play-Doh and coloring stimulates a creative mind, and even if we lick the bowl, we're still ladies. This book exemplifies all the reason we love Eckstein's books."

—Yolanda M. Johnson-Bryant, LW Media Group and author of *That Literary Lady Knows* series

"The concepts mentioned in this book allow adults ways to be open for creativity and effectiveness, but I find that for as much as I will be using these techniques myself, I will apply them in my classroom as well. Children's natural interest and curiosity combinded with their desire to play provides a great motivation to learn. I hope to fire their joy of learning, creativity, and imagination through play the way my mind has been fired after reading this book!"

—Keri M. Helgerman, MME, Intervention Specialist

"Kristen truly is able to show us the value in lemons, beach balls, frozen yogurt, our right brains, bandaids, swings, and rocks. Teaching us to remain kids at heart as we skip through our lives in this useful and fun book. A great quick read before activating the stars on the ceiling as we go to bed at night."

—Expect Miracles, Shane Belceto, CPC, InspirationalQuoteBook.com

"I help holistic entrepreneurs create the thriving businesses of their dreams, but one of the biggest problems I run into is that everyone wants to be *so serious* all the time. It's as if everyone thinks business has to be difficult and corporate and buttoned-up in a three-piece suit even if you've left that environment behind!

All entrepreneurs need to break out of their boxes and flex their creativity, and *21 Ways to be a Kid Again & Get Adult Results* gives a number of ways to do just that! Not only will these 'exercises' make your life more fun, but it will improve your business and your bottom line. Thanks for a much-needed book, Kristen. I will be recommending this to all of my clients!"

— Michelle Mahoney, Your Kick-Ass Business Coach, KickAssBusinessNews.com

"WOW! I so enjoyed this book and would love to buy copies for all of my team! I loved being a kid again, even just in my mind. You gave me so many more ideas—I'm so energized!!!"

—Pam Stegman

"What a powerful book. I don't think any of us remember when we stopped playing and creating and became adults, but Kristen's book made me realize just how much I miss it! As an author of dog books and other genre, getting 'stuck' is frustrating and time consuming. Having an arsenal of new fun tools to get my left and right brains working together is priceless!

Case in point, how to describe a somewhat complex canine interaction. Completely stuck, until I took the porcelain dog figurines (my version of action figures) on my desk and play-acted the scene! Brilliant! Those figurines have, up to this point, been only good for collecting dust. Now, thanks to Kristen's brilliant book, they are a valuable writing tool!

Do yourself a favor, purchase *21 Way To Be A Kid Again & Get Adult Results*, then find a quiet place to actually sit down and read it. It will be time and money very, very well spent. Then run, don't walk, to your nearest purveyor of toys!"

—Edie MacKenzie

"Thirty years ago I invented Sidewalk Chalk in my kitchen in Niwot, CO. Little did I ever imagine what doors that spurt of creativity would bring in to my life. I ended up opening 5 manufacturing facilities around the world to meet the marketplace demand, and during the process met the most amazing people in the toy industry. I'm thrilled to call toy giants like Bill Killgallon (Etch A Sketch), Betty James (Slinky), Pleasant Rowland (American Girl), Madam Alexander, Lane Nemeth (Discovery Toys) and so many, many more my good friends. These are adults who never lost their child-like creativity and ability to mix having fun with serious adult work.

Kristen Eckstein's book, which links missing or forgotten child-like creativity to the toys we played with in childhood, is timely and important in a world where too many of us (me included) spend too much time on computers, iPhones, and tablets. There's not a single adult who can't benefit from remembering how to have fun.

The freedom to create via play extends into our work world in ways we don't even recognize. Follow Kristen's 21 Ways and watch your world become a more free-flowing, creative, and fun—yes, *fun*—place to be.

Open up to your creative juices... you never know what may be lurking around waiting to pop out of your mind."

—Marcia Reece, inventor of world famous Sidewalk Chalk, marketing muscle for Power Rangers, author of *Secrets of the Marriage Mouse*
MarriageMouse.com

21 WAYS

to be a kid again & get adult results

Kristen Eckstein

Discover! BOOKS™
an Imprint of Imagine! Books™

High Point, North Carolina

21 Ways™ Series, Book 6

Published by Discover! Books™
an Imprint of Imagine! Books™
PO Box 16268, High Point, NC 27261
contact@artsimagine.com

Imagine! Books™ is an enterprise of Imagine! Studios™
Visit us online at www.artsimagine.com

Copyright © 2012 Kristen Eckstein
Cover Design © 2012 Imagine! Studios™
Illustrations by Drawperfect, AdrianHillman, creator76,
KeithBishop, mikessss purchased at istockphoto.com

All rights reserved. No part of this publication may be reproduced
or transmitted in any form or by any means, including informational
storage and retrieval systems, without permission in writing from
the copyright holder, except for brief quotations in a review.

ISBN 13: 978-1-937944-09-4

First Discover! Books™ printing, July 2012

Dedication

To all those who wish they could
Dance like no one is watching,
Sing like nobody's listening,
Love like you've never been hurt,
And *truly live* like there's nothing to fear.

Acknowledgements

Many thanks to:

My mother, who told me while I was growing up that I march to the beat of a different drummer than anyone else—and who loved me for it.

My husband, who regularly engages in Lego building activities with me, whom I can always count on to build sand castles and fly kites, and who knows where all the best swings are in the neighborhood.

My business coach and mentor, Bob Jenkins, who took a chance on his geeky student and let me play with a Lightsaber while speaking on his stage.

And to all my clients who appreciate the creativity I bring to their projects.

Your encouragement and ability to love me for who I am, "childlike" qualities and all, help me feel free to take risks, innovate new ideas, and inspire others. May this book be an insight into my soul and offer you inspiration to create your own amazing new ideas.

Introduction

I've seen it time and again. As kids we live life on the edge, uninhibited. One moment we're slaying dragons from the tallest tower. The next we're swinging from vines in the depths of the forest. We're loving life, having fun, and living it up in our imaginations. Then we grow up, get serious, and lose an important piece of ourselves.

So what happens? Why do we lose all that ability to take risks and be imaginative and innovative? Why does it seem that only some people, like entrepreneurs who risk their necks every day in the business world, have what it takes to create new things? To take on new challenges without a second thought? To jump into situations without knowing if they'll succeed or bounce back if they fail?

I'm one of these crazy risk-takers, and I've found a link between my childlike nature and my high level of creativity, imagination, and innovation. This book is filled with the things *I* do to tap into my own creative spirit. And I've seen these same things unleash powerful innovation in others, when they allow themselves to be kids again.

If you're "stuck," if you, like so many adults, have lost the ability to have pure unadulterated fun (without using the excuse of kids or grandkids), or if you just want to remember what it was like when you were uninhibited by "life," this book is for you.

It's time for you to be a kid again. And experience adult results!

Swing!

Much of my childhood was spent outdoors in one of two places: on the beach (see Way 15) or on my tire swing. My happiest and most lively moments were spent on that swing, and to this day a swing set is one of my best friends. Or a porch swing. Or a hammock. Heck, if it moves in a swing-like fashion and I'm within twenty feet of it, you can bet I'll be spending some quality time on it. A *lot* of quality time.

Swinging is one of the few "exercises" (yes, it counts!) we can do that bring back the mindset of childhood. Almost immediately, as your brain soars and your stomach flops, you'll begin to reminisce about a simpler time, a time when you didn't care what other people thought. You just wanted to have fun. A time when your ideas flowed freely and your imagination put you in impossible situations only the mind of a child could invent—and rescue you from.

The magical thing about swings is that their creative effect still works for adults! Some of my best ideas come about when I'm on a swing letting my mind wander and my spirit soar. In fact, the *21 Ways* series was born on my porch swing late at night when my brain was so fatigued I couldn't even think anymore. All I could do was push myself back and forth, and right when I was completely relaxed, this book series idea popped into my head. And this particular book, *21 Ways to Be a Kid Again & Get Adult Results*, came about when I was swinging at a park after a seven-mile bicycle ride, gazing up at the clouds as they came fully into view and imagining them to be mythical creatures of doom (see Way 6).

Swinging can truly unleash all sorts of creativity typically kept bottled up inside your soul. But one thing can inhibit this unleashing—caring what other people think. Any life coach, counselor, or psychiatrist will tell you that caring about what other people think about you causes you to become self-conscious, depressed, overly OCD, and worse—you lose your will to take risks and create.

It doesn't matter if you're all grown up and "sophisticated," you can still enjoy simple pastimes such as swings. And if you get weird looks from other adults, know this: Most of them are probably just jealous they don't have the guts to not care what other people think. Most of them secretly wish they were soaring up to the skies and plummeting to the earth alongside you. In that moment, most of them *wish they were you*. So go ahead—*be you* and swing like no one is watching!

WAY 2

Sculpt Play-Doh

As I write this book, I have a blob of goo passing between my fingers. There's just something in the mindless action of sculpting an amorphous material that activates the neural fibers (corpus callosum for you science geeks reading this book) between the left and right brain, activating the right brain and allowing it to create, write, and generate ideas.

Think about kids that play with Play-Doh. They come up with the most amazing creations (my favorite was making pizza). Imaginations run wild when kids play with Play-Doh—for good reason! When the left brain is analyzing, the right brain is silent. One of the only ways to make the pathway between the hemispheres open communication is to do a mindless activity, like rolling Play-Doh between your hands. This mindless activity causes the creative side of the right brain to spark, and before you know it you're creating snakes, cubes, stacks, snowmen, balls, spirals, and more complex shapes. You can easily get lost in play, which is perfectly OK. When you're completely absorbed in play, your right brain is free to imagine. And imagination is what brings innovation. And innovation solves complex problems and creates amazing new products that help countless numbers of people.

If you can't handle the thought of giving in to the child inside you and buying some Play-Doh, consider getting some Thinking Putty, which is basically adult Play-Doh, or Silly Putty on steroids. ThinkGeek.com has the best selection of Thinking Putty I've ever seen (see Way 18 for more that ThinkGeek.com has to offer) and I'm particularly partial to the variety Magnetic Black Hole. Just keep it away from your computer or other sensitive electronics! Thinking Putty has a stiffer consistency to Play-Doh, however, so it can be harder to work.

There's also another option if you don't want the stiffer variety of Thinking Putty or if you have food allergies or celiac disease (as I do), which eliminates Play-Doh as a "safe" substance. Get yourself some Crayola Model Magic. This is a very soft, pliable gluten-free material that holds its soft shape so you can allow your creations to dry. Hey, you might create something you want to show off to the kids!

So now you have no more excuses. Next time you get stuck trying to brainstorm a solution to a problem or a new idea for a project, I challenge you to grab a can of your chosen putty and start rolling it around in your hands. You might be surprised how quickly fresh ideas begin to come.

Resources in this Way:

 Play-Doh

 Crayola Model Magic

 Thinking Putty

Go on a Treasure Hunt

I was recently introduced to this "adult" activity that truly makes you feel like a big kid going on an adventure. Geocaching is a fun treasure-hunting experience that has a side effect of showing you places nearby you never knew existed.

How it works

Caches have been hidden all over your neighborhood. There are literally millions of them around the world, and all you have to do is find them! They can be "micro" in size, like the size of a sample perfume bottle, or large like a shoebox. They are usually camouflaged containers to keep nosy people out, and, if they're located in a place where they might get wet from rain, the contents are usually placed in plastic bags. The goal is to find a cache, enter your name and the date in the logbook, and, if the cache allows for small trinkets, you can add or trade one for something that you like. Here are the steps to go on a Geocache mission:

Step 1

First, sign up at Geocaching.com for a free account. Then if you have a smart phone, download the Geocaching app. There's a free app that works great for beginners, but if you start to get addicted you might want to go for the paid app as it has a lot of features the free one doesn't offer.

Step 2

Start up the app and follow the steps to choose a cache. The free app has a nice little introduction on how to locate caches near you. Once you choose a cache to find, drive, bike, or walk to the location on the map on your phone. You can also use the compass to guide you closer.

Step 3

Once you're at the designated coordinates in the cache listing, start looking. Look behind fallen trees, under rocks, inside bridge supports, inside light pole bases—look anywhere a camouflaged container might be able to hide. Keep in mind the compass may get you close, but not exactly to the cache. There will be some "hunting" involved to find this treasure!

Step 4

Once you've found the cache, open it! You never know what you might find. It could be really useful stuff or a bunch of junk. It could be toys or batteries. It could also be so small it can only hold a logbook.

Step 5

Sign the logbook with your name (or your Geocaching.com screen name), bundle it all back up and hide it back where you found it. Then if you have the time, go find another cache!

My husband and I recently went on a Geocaching mission at a nearby park we've been to several times before. This cache was off a greenway, up a footpath, across a creek, and up farther through a streambed to a big flat rock surrounded by flowering cacti. After a bit of hunting, we found the cache. Then we went back down to the creek and sat on a rock overlooking a waterfall. I took that opportunity to wade in the creek (see Way 5) and have a little more kidlike fun. We would never have known this place existed if we hadn't been hunting for the cache, and it's definitely a site we'll visit again!

One final note: Caches can be labeled as "night" caches or daytime caches. They can also be part of a series, where one cache leads to clues of where the next can be found. The best part about Geocaching is that it gets you out doing something you probably dreamed of doing as a kid—going on a treasure hunt! So get out of the office, get some friends together, and go have fun!

Resources in this Way:

 Geocaching.com

Build Something with Legos

Almost all of us had Legos when we were kids. We'd spend countless hours connecting blocks to create an endless supply of hand-built wonders. Our imaginations ran wild as we placed green blocks over blue blocks over red blocks over yellow blocks, completing our masterpieces with sets of wheels and a Lego minifigure in all his stylized glory towering at the top to drive this new masterpiece off a make-believe cliff.

Legos are toys that require a healthy imagination. If you've ever been to a Lego store and seen the giant figures created with tiny Lego blocks, you've probably asked yourself, "How do they *do* that?" The answer is a factory where people play with Legos all day long. These people must have healthy imaginations in order to keep their jobs—and keep coming up with fantastic Lego kits for us to buy.

OK, I'll admit that I actually applied for a position at such a place when I was in college. Apparently a lot of adults wanted to relive their childhoods, so competition was fierce and I didn't get the position. Or it could be because I was in college and the job was in a town two hours away. Despite that, playing with Legos has become a standard activity in my house and I've found it to be a way to get out of my analytical mind and break free of the barriers of conventional thought.

The best part about playing with Legos is that there's no wrong answer. You can make *anything you want* and no one will make fun of you because it's the wrong thing. If you have trouble allowing yourself to play with these toys on your own, find a kid and play with him or her for a little while. Sometimes it takes being with a kid to tap into the child inside you that's starving for attention. You don't need the excuse of having kids around to be one yourself, but you may need to work up to giving yourself that permission. But I encourage you to eventually give yourself permission by buying a small kit of Legos for yourself and playing with them—by yourself—on a regular basis.

Your ultimate goal should be to let all your analytical thought patterns loose and just *create*. When you truly let your imagination run free—just as you did when you were a kid—you'll find yourself coming up with more extravagant, silly creations. Believe there are no limits and you'll unlock a part of your brain that's been dormant for years. That part of your brain will help you access solutions to problems you may have been struggling with for quite some time. And you just might create something fun in the meantime.

WAY 5

Wade Barefoot

Do you remember hot summer days when you were a kid? Did you ever throw your shoes and socks off and jump into a creek or stream, splashing and laughing as you went? Then you grew up and gazed upon those streams from a distance, reminiscing about your childhood.

What happened? Why does growing up mean we can't splash in streams anymore? For me, the ability to let all my worries go and splash around in a stream does wonders to lift my spirits and clear my mind. And I bet it would do the same for you, too.

The key to make wading in a stream work for helping your mind clear is to pick a stream that runs fairly cold (there's nothing like a jolt of cold water to wake up your brain) and focus on little things that keep you in the moment. We've all heard the saying, "stop and smell the roses," but do we really *know* what that means? To me it means living in the moment. Feeling, really *feeling*, the cold of the water, the current flowing around your legs, and the sand between your toes is how you can truly begin to live *in the moment*.

So here's my challenge to you. Next time you're near a stream, whether it's on a hike, while camping, or riding your bike along a trail, do yourself a favor and stop to savor a splash. Take off your shoes and socks and jump into that fresh, chilly water. Dare to have a little fun and not care what others around you may think. Wade out to a rock in the middle of the stream and perch atop it while hunting for fish in the water below. Splash someone standing on the shore and start a mini water fight. Feel the sand or stones beneath your feet and how the water rushes between your toes. Breathe in the healthy, fresh air and savor the smells of nature.

Cool your body temperature and relax. And above all, focus on living *in the moment*. The resulting mental clarity you will gain is worth the risk in daring to be a kid again.

Cloud Dreaming

Imagine you're lying flat on your back, gazing up at the sky. Full, white, puffy clouds are floating, drifting, and changing shape before your eyes.

Forget about the science of cloud formation at the moment. What do you see? Do you see a mass of liquid droplets or frozen water molecules suspended in the atmosphere above the Earth? Or do you see beyond, to another realm, to something more?

I bet if you did this prior to eighth grade physical science class, you *always* saw something more. In fact, back then your right brain wasn't severely damaged by facts, figures, and responsibilities, so you probably saw more than you're able to now—at least until you're done reading this Way.

Let me start by telling you what I see.

I see a T-Rex morphing into a rubber ducky. I see a dragon with a huge tail blowing fire at a city on a hill. I see grand stories playing themselves out in the sky above, beckoning me to observe and to delight in their messages. I see the facts of science giving way to the miracles of possibility. And I see creativity being infused from the clouds through my eyes, my skin, my pores, until it becomes the core, the very essence, of who I am.

Now I'll ask you again. What do you *see?* Do you still see cumulous masses of gas floating in the sky above? Or do you see something more? Do you see scientific fact? Or do you see possibility?

Seeing the stories in the clouds is one easy way to give your right brain permission to fully open, fully engage, and throw off the confines of factual adulthood. When you can see those stories in the clouds, problems will fade away and solutions will magically present themselves.

If you're having trouble with this exercise, try this:

Step 1: Go outside and either sit or lie down on the ground, or sit where you can easily see the sky.

Step 2: Close your eyes and take a deep breath. Hold it in for seven seconds, and then let it out in four. Do this three times, breathing so that your stomach expands and your shoulders don't rise. (Hint: If you've never practiced breathing, try this in a mirror first so you see what it looks like. Also see the book *21 Ways to Run a Stress-Free Business* by Dr. Daisy Sutherland for information on how to properly take "cleansing" breaths.)

Step 3: Open your eyes and gaze at the clouds. Nothing may come to you at first, but don't get discouraged. The cleansing breaths from Step 2 should have helped empty your mind (aka your analytical left brain), so there may be nothing there right away. As you watch the clouds pass overhead, envision what they may look like. What's happening in the drama above you?

As you take these steps, your imagination should begin to roam uninhibited. Even if you can only spare five minutes, next time you're outside, take a little extra time to "cloud dream." You may be surprised at the creative results you'll get from letting go of your thoughts and envisioning magical beings in the clouds.

And right now, I see a mass of pending doom as dark thunderstorm clouds come my way, threatening me to vacate my swing (see Way 1) and head back into the safety of shelter. Don't worry, if weather doesn't permit you to cloud dream, there are plenty of things you can do inside to stimulate your creativity, such as sculpting Play-Doh (Way 2), playing with Legos (Way 4), walking a Slinky down a flight of stairs (Way 13), coloring (Way 17), and a few other gems in this book I'll let you discover on your own.

WAY 7

Learn from Disney

They don't call it "the happiest place on Earth" for no reason! Disney World for East Coast folks or Disneyland for those venturing to the West Coast are two of the few places adults can go and experience what it's like to be a kid all over again. And there's nothing like heading to Disney without the responsibility of children to throw off the chains of adult responsibilities and truly enjoy yourself.

It may sound mean, and chances are if you have kids and they find out you went to Disney without them, they'll probably be mad at you for months on end. But you're the adult, and the magical thing about being an adult and tapping into your kidlike side is that you *don't have to tell them!*

My husband and I have made visiting Disney World a regular occurrence. It's one of the few places I can act like a kid, show childlike excitement, and get no shameful looks of "you should know better" from others. In fact, reactions are quite to the contrary in the magical world of Disney. Everyone there seems enraptured by the new ability to cast off restraint and *simply enjoy* the experience.

There are no adults telling you to tone it down or hold in your excitement. As Aladdin put it so eloquently, there's "no one to tell us 'no,' or where to go, or say we're only dreaming." I think Disney's onto something.

Think about it: Many of Disney's animated movies are stories of adult characters wanting something more, something magical. Think about Belle longing for "much more than this provincial life" or Arial wishing to be part of a different world. In each story, the hero or heroine triumphs over some form of evil (I personally see it as the boring, mundane, "responsible" adult life) to see his or her dreams come true in a completely magical way. And, of course, each magical transformation is usually accompanied by a song.

Why can't it be that way in real life? Why can't we infuse every potentially tedious task with fun and creative energy? Why does emptying the dishwasher have to be a task we *need* to get done rather than a game? Why can't we simply sing a song and watch our to-do lists evaporate before our eyes? If you have kids, you may have made a game out of cleaning their room to encourage them to clean it. They had fun and you got what you wanted—a clean room. But have we ever thought about applying these *games* to our own chores?

If you can't make it to Disney World without the kids, think of how you can bring the wonder of Disney to your world. What can you do to change *how* you do something to bring a sense of magic and fun into it? It's true we should be responsible. We have bills to pay and mouths to feed. But that doesn't mean we have to give up fun, wonder, and magic. Sometimes getting those bills paid *requires* magic! In fact, I'll be so bold as to say every mundane task we do can have a new sense of energy if we simply apply a little magic to it.

Next time you're working on a routine task, think about Cinderella washing the floors or Belle feeding the chickens. Think about Giselle from *Enchanted* singing the "Happy Working Song" while cleaning "crud up in the kitchen" with her vermin friends. What song can you sing to breathe life, energy, and magic into the task? When you can accomplish this, you'll be amazed at how much faster these tasks get done and how much more time will magically appear in your day!

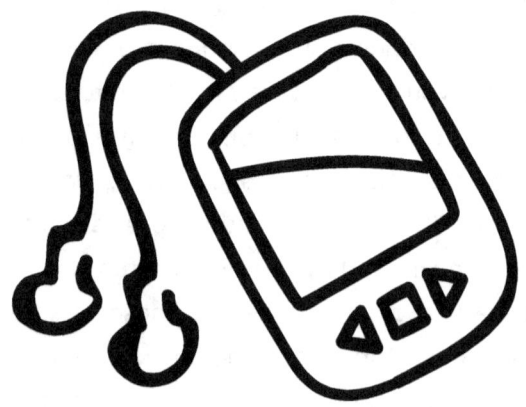

Cartoon Band-Aids

It was almost eight o'clock last night and I was exhausted from a full day of nonstop phone meetings. My husband was in the kitchen slicing vegetables and I was resting on the couch. I didn't even realize I'd fallen asleep until I jolted awake to the sounds of panic coming from the kitchen.

And instantly I knew what had happened—Joe had cut himself. And it hurt. *Bad.* Thankfully it wasn't deep and he got it under cold running water to cleanse and numb it, but it reminded me of a very important fact: As adults, we still hurt ourselves.

We still fall down and skin our knees, get in accidents, and, more times than we ought to, we rush through life and end up with nasty cuts on our fingers. Unlike when we were kids, once we're grown there's no one to bandage us up except ourselves. And usually we reach for the boring flesh-colored bandages we found on sale at the local drugstore in an effort to hide and protect our wounds.

No longer do we proudly sport Spiderman bandages that cheer us up. No more do Tom and Jerry make us smile as they chase each other around our wounds. The Roadrunner has long since run away; He-Man and She-Ra are off fighting battles in another universe; and we're left with dull tan strips to grace our cuts as we go on with our "adult" responsibilities.

To me, hiding behind our invisible bandages is a big problem. Especially if your wounds are emotional, it's hard for others to see when you're hurting and need help. No matter how many times we tell ourselves, "I'm an adult, I can get my own boring band-aid and hide my pain," the fact is that *we need each other*. We were designed to be in relationship with each other, to support each other through rough days, to be surrounded by love when the wounds seem to go so deep we're not sure if we'll survive.

Something most people don't know about me is that, during the summer of 2011, I almost took my own life—more than once. I felt like I had to put on a happy face and not let anyone know what I was going through. I had three friends who knew most of what was happening in my life, but even they didn't know the true extent of it. I even broke down in tears *on a stage* at an event where I was speaking because I couldn't hold the turmoil in any longer.

One of the things that got me through was opening myself up to friends on Facebook. Most of my Facebook friends seemed to think I always magically had everything together, when the fact was I'd almost followed through on ending my own life the very day I posted something happy and upbeat.

Finally, one day I had it. I was hurting and at last I got sick of trying to hide behind my flesh-colored band-aid. I said enough is enough and I posted a short post about how I was *really* feeling. And you know what happened? No one condemned me for not being perfect. No one unfriended me because I was having a rough time. In fact, I was completely blown away by the support I received.

Within *minutes* I had dozens of comments. People supporting me, loving me, and some people thanking me for giving them permission to reach out to others when they were hurting and not hide behind their "I've got it all together" Internet personas anymore.

Those people changed my life that day. And in turn, I changed some others. That post got the most comments of anything I've ever posted to Facebook before or since. That should tell us something!

We've been trained to hide when we get hurt, to sulk in a corner and lick our wounds alone, to "suck it up" and not let our friends, Facebook or otherwise, know we're having a rough day. And I must ask, "*Why?*" Why is it unacceptable to show we're vulnerable? Why must we always be super heroes? Why can't we show we're human, admit we're having a rough time, and be bold enough to ask for help with bandaging our wounds?

Well, I say, "No more!" There's nothing that makes you feel better when you're hurting than a brightly colored cartoon bandage. Instead of trying to hide the fact that we got hurt, we *can* choose to proudly proclaim to the world, "Yes, I still get injured. I'm an adult and I'm not afraid to let others know I'm human—just like them. I still get hurt, and I'm proud to wear Nemo on my finger because, gosh darn it, he makes me feel good!"

So next time you're at the store picking up bandages, reach for some brightly colored fun characters. Let them be a reminder that you don't need to be ashamed of getting hurt. You *can* let others know how you feel and give them the chance to support you through those difficult times.

Now if you'll excuse me, I need to go find a Kermit the Frog bandage for my husband's finger.

Bike for Fun

Exercise. It's a concept we know well and one we often loathe. In January every year, thousands of people make one single resolution: to get fit. As a society in the United States, we eat too much, sit too much, and watch our celebrities' belly fat get Photoshopped away as an example of what we should strive to look like.

Our Facebook streams are inundated with pictures and inspirational quotes about wellness and exercise, and we gaze at them as our rear ends conform even more to our computer chairs. And we think to ourselves, *I'll make time for the gym tomorrow.*

The fact is, most people cancel their shiny new gym memberships after a class or two, in the month of March, or when life gets too busy to make time for the gym and they can't justify that added expense each month. Health and wellness is a billion dollar industry filled with millions of people gaining more weight each year.

If the industry is so popular and exercise is spoken about so much, why aren't more people successful at keeping up their exercise regimens?

I think it's because exercise is no longer *play*. When we were kids, we'd do cartwheels (see Way 16), run around the neighborhood, swing on swings at the park (see Way 1), ride bikes up and down the street, hula hoop (see Way 12), dance to our favorite music (see Way 21), and always, *always* have fun doing it. We burned massive calories without knowing what it was we were even doing.

Then we grew up, got a job sitting at a computer for eight hours straight each day, noticed our clothes weren't fitting as well anymore, got a gym membership (because that's what adults do), and cancelled it a few months later due to lack of time and decreased interest.

So what did we do at this point? We bought a treadmill and stuck it in the basement. After all, it was on sale, promised to shed pounds *fast,* and was much cheaper than a gym membership—once we used it for a full year.

Six months later we walk into the basement room and gaze on our once-promising treadmill standing tall, and count the number of spiders who have made it their permanent home. And we turn off the light, turn our backs to our failure to exercise, and list the treadmill on Craigslist.

Why do we keep spending money on exercise memberships and equipment that don't last more than a few months? Why can't we keep up with it no matter how hard we try? I believe it's because somewhere along the way, exercise quit being "play" and turned into work. It's a solitary act unless we join special classes that only last a short time. It's repetitive and lacks variety. It's something we "have to do" to stay healthy. In short, it's *work*. No wonder we hate doing it!

It's time we changed our mindsets toward exercise. Instead of spending thirty minutes on the treadmill, take a walk with a loved one around your neighborhood. Visit a local state park and hike to a waterfall. Take a ride on your bike just to feel the wind blow around you and the rush of speed under your feet. Do outdoor (or indoor) physical activities with *fun* as the goal—with *play* in mind. Quit calling it "exercise" and start calling it "playtime."

Instead of making exercise—err, playtime—a part of your routine of to-dos for the week, make it an exciting and engaging activity you'll look forward to doing. In short, *make it fun*. Making it fun can be different things to different people. If you're competitive by nature, it can mean competing with a friend to see who can ride the most miles on a bicycle in a week. If you like taking time to enjoy the beauty of nature, it could mean hiking a mountain or kayaking down a stream. If you enjoy learning new things, take a chance and enroll in horseback riding or martial arts classes. Whatever makes you engage with the mindset of *play*, do it at least once a week.

Even if you choose to keep your gym membership or dust the cobwebs off that treadmill in the basement, mixing up your routine to include *play*ful activities will bring a new energy and excitement to your life. And if you find yourself hanging clothes to dry on that freshly dusted treadmill, perhaps it's time for another change. Re-read this Way and get out and *play!*

WAY 10

Lick the Bowl

Have you ever had the urge to do something completely crazy, then stopped yourself with the thought, *"but what if somebody sees me?"* I thought so. We all have. As kids we had no problem acting on a whim, doing whatever popped into our minds without thinking first.

Then society told us that's not a good idea. "Think before you act" is the command drilled into us over and over again. And although it's not a bad idea to think before you act, it has other repercussions those well-meaning people didn't understand.

Suddenly we become self-conscious and overly concerned with what others think about us. We stop taking action and start revising, then revising some more, then revising even more to get it "just right" before exposing anything to the world.

If you've ever tried to write a book, you've experienced this overdeveloped sense of perfectionism. Your manuscript will sit on your hard drive and collect virtual dust for years as you continue to make sure it's "perfect" for fear of what others may think. In fact, in my survey for aspiring authors at JumpstartMyBook.com, the number one fear people put down isn't money for publishing and marketing, it isn't time to write their books, which I thought would be more common. No, the number one fear is fear of rejection from their readers.

Because somewhere along the way, what others think started to dictate our choices, our ideas, and before we knew it, our very *lives*. And this leads to something even worse.

Fewer projects get completed. More books are left unwritten (see my book *21 Ways to Write & Publish Your Non-Fiction Book* for more help in this area). Vast numbers of inspiring quotations are shared in social media by people living vicariously through those who *took action* on their dreams and accomplished something. And more of those people sharing those quotations are doing nothing to accomplish their own dreams.

This is a problem! Your dream, your message, your project, your book are meant to be shared. As my business coach Bob the Teacher Jenkins points out in his book, you need to *Take Action! Revise Later*.

There is one surefire way I know of to beat the "what they think about me" syndrome. To lick the bowl. Next time you go out to eat for dinner, order ice cream for dessert or stop at a popular ice cream parlor before you head home. When you're finished eating, before throwing your bowl or cup away, lick it. That's right: *Lick* it. In public. In front of other people.

Do something crazy despite what others "may think" about you. Lick that bowl. I always lick the bowl. And I can tell you from experience, that simple (yet somehow so hard to follow through with) activity forces those thoughts of, "but what might they think about me?" out of my mind. There is freedom when you quit focusing on what others "may think" about you and start focusing on what *you* want.

And sometimes what you want, what you really desire, is to do something crazy *without the fear* of what others may think. Something like licking an ice cream bowl in public. So go ahead, lick the bowl. Do these small crazy things often enough and, before you know it, you'll be taking action on projects and not worrying about whether or not they're perfect. And the world will be a better place for what you're giving to it!

Resources in this Way:

JumpstartMyBook.com
aspiring author survey

21 Ways to Write & Publish Your Non-Fiction Book
by Kristen Eckstein

Take Action! Revise Later
by Bob the Teacher Jenkins

WAY 11

Beach Ball Brainstorming

According to a study by the American Psychological Association, "groups perform better than the best individuals at solving complex problems." Our brains are designed to feed off the thoughts and ideas of others as we face our own challenges. This is why teamwork on projects in school and business mastermind groups are so popular. The experts in charge of these organized brainstorming sessions understand the way our brains can take one thought from someone else and develop it into a complete solution for whatever we may be working on.

I've taken this one step further to incorporate the element of play and right-brain activity. Psychologists have discovered that the right brain (creative side) is continuously hungry for attention and demandss satisfaction. In order for the right brain to process ideas and solutions, the path between the normally dominant left brain and the demanding, yet usually unsatisfied, right brain must be opened. Only then can the right brain find creative solutions to problems and generate ideas that the left brain can then implement.

Often while coaching my clients, I come up with ideas they never thought of, more often than not surprising myself in the process. When I found out about the science between right and left brain interaction and creative problem solving, a light bulb went on in my mind as to why I've never had trouble coming up with solutions to creativity problems. After I read the book *Write. 10 Days to Overcome Writer's Block. Period.* by Karen E. Peterson, Ph.D., I learned about the art of satisfying the right brain and the science of right and left working together. And that's when the magic happens.

I regularly tell people the toys in my office are for *me* and I use them for problem solving and generating creative ideas. The truth is I just refuse to grow up. Discovering this creative connection was more of an accident than anything intentional. As I studied more on this right-left brain issue, I came up with an activity that has become a must-do in my office any time we're stuck trying to find a solution to a problem. I call it Beach Ball Brainstorming.

Beach Ball Brainstorming is a simple three-step process:

Step 1: Buy a beach ball

Head over to your local discount store and get a beach ball. It's the best $2 investment for your right brain you will ever make.

Step 2: Blow it up

A beach ball folded in its original packaging and sitting on a forgotten closet shelf will get you nowhere. Buying it isn't enough. You have to open that package and blow it up! This also gets you breathing deeply, which will loosen you up for Step 3.

Step 3: Toss and talk

This can be done two ways: with a friend or against a wall. You'll want to toss your new beach ball in a way that it will come back to you so you can keep tossing it. It's easier with a friend, and even better with someone who knows a little about the issue you want to brainstorm, as having that additional set of ideas will help generate more of your own. If you prefer to work alone, toss it against a wall where it will bounce back and just start talking. You might feel silly talking to yourself, but then you already look silly tossing a beach ball around by yourself, so what have you got to lose?

Here's why it works: Your right brain is like a demanding 3-year-old who's rarely satisfied. By engaging the right brain in play and brainstorming the problem with the left brain, the pathways between the two are opened and creative solutions are able to flow freely from right to left. If we do not satisfy the right brain's need for play, that connection is closed off and every time we try to solve our creative issue, it feels like an uphill battle. We constantly hit brick walls because the right brain is the hub of problem solving. By "starving" it of what it needs, we inhibit its ability to help us in our time of need. This is why Beach Ball Brainstorming is so effective.

This technique has been used successfully in my office for brainstorming new project ideas, how to handle particularly sticky client situations, and for solving creative problems such as when we're stuck on a chapter of a book or the dialogue of a cartoon. I have even started incorporating it into my workshops and seen attendees get dramatic results. In the first workshop in which I used this method, an attendee was struggling with a book idea. She didn't think she could write a book because she had been stuck on how to move forward with her idea for three *years*. After less than ten minutes with me and a beach ball, she left my workshop with complete outlines for *two* different books and an outline for an entire eBook *series*.

In fact, her Beach Ball Brainstorming experience paved the way for me to create another workshop completely around this idea of play and right-left brain connection, *Righting Your Left Brain: How to Break the Constraints on Your Creativity & Open the Door to Creative Problem Solving* (see

BookCoachMedia.com/topics for more information about that workshop).

As this example shows, Beach Ball Brainstorming can have a huge positive impact on your creativity. If you don't already have a beach ball, go complete Steps 1 and 2 above and repeat Step 3 as needed. Have fun discovering some surprising solutions to your creative blocks!

Resources in this Way:

 *Write. 10 Days to Overcome Writer's Block. Period.* by Karen E. Peterson, Ph.D.

 Right Your Left Brain Workshop

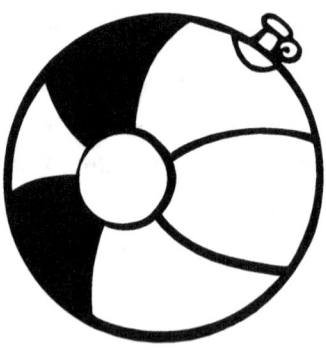

WAY 12

Hula Hoop

If you enjoy crazy YouTube videos, look up "Masha Silaeva - Cirque de Soleil - Hula Hoop." When I first saw that video, I was mesmerized for the entire four minutes. I kept wondering how many hours' worth of practice went into her hula hoop routine. If you've ever tried to hula hoop, you know keeping that ring spinning around your waist takes a specific combination of balance, rocking back and forth, and hip swinging. It takes *practice* to keep that hoop from dropping to the ground.

This is the same in everything we do in life. If you expect to do something perfectly the first time you try your hand at it, you're in for a severe reality check when you get poor results. I see this often in my business when aspiring authors think they can design a book cover just as well as our professional book designers who have years of experience. They expect to get the same results with their book as authors who publish with a mainstream traditional publishing house, and they're sorely disappointed when they find out the opposite is true. Any book coach worth his salt will tell authors they can't edit their own work or design their own books, and expect to get the same results as those who hire professionals. Because coaches understand practice makes perfect, and most authors have never practiced in these areas.

Professionals in any field have practiced, experimented over and over, and discovered what works, what doesn't, and why. They know how to get the results their clients desire and can usually accomplish their clients' goals in a fraction of the time it would take their clients to learn by trial, error, and much frustration how to do it themselves.

If you're a professional or expert in your field, you probably reached that level the same way. You experimented, found what worked and what didn't, tweaked, revised, and finally created something that can benefit those around you. Whether you're the head of a team at a corporation and have discovered how to get your team to achieve their goals, or you're the owner of a small business and figured out what your clients will pay good money to hire you for, you have achieved these things through practice. And that practice came at a great price of time and money (if you took classes to gain that expertise).

If you want to become a proficient hula-hooper, practice spinning a hula hoop. Besides being a ton of fun, the persistence required to keep the hoop up can be applied to perfecting your skills in your work. Determine to be the best _____ you can be in your field, and practice hard to reach that point. Know your value, know your investment of becoming the expert you are, don't undermine yourself, and above all, *don't quit*. Keep practicing, because eventually, practice makes perfect.

WAY 13

Slinky

I'm now humming the Slinky theme song to myself. Can you remember it? "It's Slinky, it's Slinky, for fun it's a wonderful toy. It's Slinky, it's Slinky, it's fun for a girl and a boy." Did you have a Slinky when you were a kid? If you did, I'm sure at some point you sent it tumbling down a flight of stairs. After all, walking down stairs is what Slinky is famous for. And if you have sent a Slinky to walk down a flight of stairs, you also know many times Slinky takes a wrong step and either rolls a bit or comes to a complete stand-still. And that, of course, is not what you intended for it to do.

Life won't always let everything go your way. Sometimes the local pizza place runs out of pepperoni right when you get seated and order.

Sometimes the short line at the grocery store ends up taking twice as long as any other line. Sometimes you hit all the red lights on your way to a meeting when you're already running late. Often we call it Murphy's Law, and almost always we let these happenings get on our nerves.

I recently attended a Radical Leadership retreat founded and facilitated by Therese Kienast, and it was there that I finally realized what it means to be flexible. What became amazing to me was that, when we're flexible, it's much harder to get bent out of shape. When we're not attached to the outcome of a situation, everything ends up working out, often better than we thought it could.

When we're aware to what's happening in us, through us, and around us, we encounter less stressful "surprises" and a sense of peace and calm begins to fill every moment of our lives. And when we tap into what makes us "tick," what gets us excited and passionate, we learn how to truly live "in the moment" and we finally understand what it means to "stop and smell the roses."

Like a Slinky, our lives take a specific shape as we grow. Our flexibility in how we handle things that come up or don't quite go our way enhances our abilities instead of bending us out of shape. If it weren't for the Slinky's ability to be flexible and go with the force we put on it, it would never be able to walk down the stairs and give us hours of continuous enjoyment.

If you find yourself getting stressed out or upset when things don't go your way, I encourage you to get a Slinky. Toss it down the stairs a few times and watch its flexibility lend itself to adapt to its position and situation, yet hold its shape intact. It won't always do what you want it to (i.e., everything may not always go your way), but when you let loose and simply enjoy the process you will find that sense of calm and relaxation, and you'll find yourself impulsively smiling at whatever life—or your Slinky—sends your way.

Resources in this Way:

 Get your own classic Slinky

WAY 14

Sand Castles & Snowmen

Sometimes it rains on your parade. Sometimes a snowstorm hits and the kids' school gets canceled when you need to make it to an important meeting. Sometimes the water at the beach is too cold to swim in or the rip tides are unsafe and you're stuck on the hot sand. You've heard it before: When life gives you lemons, make lemonade.

But that is often easier said than done. When that snowstorm hits, we begin calling sitters like crazy and find no one wants to head out in the storm or we wonder why they didn't salt the street to make it easier for us to get out of our neighborhood. When we're looking forward to swimming at the beach and the water temperature or rip tides make it difficult or impossible, we gripe, complain, and decide we need shopping therapy instead at the local beach shop. We feel better for a while, until we see the credit card bill.

Why do we believe in making lemonade out of lemons, but we're always out of sugar when the lemons are thrown at us? Why do we throw temper tantrums when something interferes with our plans and try to throw the lemons back at life instead of savoring their flavor?

We may never understand exactly why this paradox exists, but I feel it's because we forget to notice what's around us. What's around you in a snowstorm? Snow. What surrounds you at the beach? Sand. So what if we quit trying to find a way around our predicaments and worked *with* the unwelcome situation instead?

What if instead of trying to get to that important meeting through a dangerous snowstorm, when the person you were meeting probably can't make it either, you choose to bundle up with the kids and enjoy building a snowman? Then you can come indoors and warm up with hot cocoa and warm fuzzy blankets. Doesn't that sound better than griping about the snow?

What if instead of racking up your credit card bill at the local beach shop, you choose to enjoy the warmth of the sun and sand and have some good old-fashioned fun building a sand castle?

To me, the choice of playing in the snow or sand quenches the desire to throw a temper tantrum and makes me excited about the prospect of working *with* the "unfortunate" situation instead. Stress melts away and peace settles in when we stop butting heads with life and start *choosing* to enjoy whatever life sends our way.

And that's the secret: choice. You have the choice to use what you've got (lemons) to create something exciting, new, different, and wonderful. You also have the choice to be miserable sucking on lemons with no sugar. Either way, the choice is yours. I know which one I'm going to start choosing!

WAY 15

Go Fly a Kite!

The weather was perfect; the waves were serene; the white sand was soft between my toes and not too hot; the beach shop was full of fun trinkets begging to come home with me; and the sounds of the surf were beckoning me into the ocean. But one single item in that beach shop rounded out my day to make it the absolute *perfect* day at the beach: a kite.

The breeze was ideal for kite flying and I really wanted a kite. The beach shop happened to have one left that appealed to my inner geek (it wasn't pink), and I picked it up for a mere $3 and took it out toward the waves. The next hour, my husband and I watched the sunset as the space shuttle on my kite danced toward the waiting stars. And

I must say, we were the envy of many "proper" adults walking by, which got me thinking.

You've probably heard the old cliché, "the sky's the limit," but what does that really mean? The truth we often hear is that we can't be everything we want to be; we can't do anything we want to do whenever we want to do it. Often we have physical limits to what is possible. Sometimes someone's holding the other end of our kite's string. But what would happen if those limits were broken? What would it be like to soar free of a tether, caught high in the wind?

In the case of the kite (and ourselves), it might crash to the ground. Or it might soar free and flow wherever the wind takes it, exploring new places and seeing incredible things it couldn't see from the ground.

Strings aren't bad. After all, without the string on my kite, I wouldn't be able to enjoy flying it or save it for another day at the beach. But in the case of our lives, strings can be a safety net that keeps us from taking risks and exploring our limits, or worse, someone else can be hanging onto your string, holding you down and keeping you from achieving your dreams. These types of people will only let you get so far toward your dream before they jerk you back again.

Here's a little secret: The one holding your string is the one you gave it to. You have the power to choose who holds it and how far you soar!

I ask you now to examine your inner kite and your string. Who are you allowing to hold it? Who has a pair of scissors that can cut it? And if it were cut, just how high do you think you could fly? What would the rush feel like? What would it be like to soar with the excitement of completing a new project you never dreamed you could finish? What if the impossible were suddenly possible? How would you feel if you were surrounded by positive, upbeat people who let go of your string just to see how far you could go, while cheering for you as you flew away?

What if you could live each day as though your strings were cut and *anything* were possible? I bet you would learn some things about yourself you never knew, and you would be happier, less stressed, and more buzzed about life than ever before!

It's time for you to let go and take a chance. Pick a goal you've always wanted to achieve and *go for it*. Take a risk. Cut your string. Go fly *your* kite!

WAY 16

Spontaneous Cartwheels

When was the last time you did something completely spontaneous? Like dance in the rain or turn a cartwheel in front of a bunch of people in a park? In my own completely humble opinion, life is dull without a little spontaneity thrown in the mix. For most people, day in and day out is always the same: Wake up, coffee, shower, brush teeth, go to work, lunch break (if you're lucky), come home, dinner, TV, bed. Rinse and repeat. Once in a while we might throw a vacation in just to mix things up a bit. But then a week later it's back to our mundane cookie-cutter lives.

What would the result be if each of us did one—just one—spontaneous thing each day? What if you acted "on a whim" once a week and did something completely out of the ordinary?

My husband, the careful analytical planner, often has trouble with this concept. He's been wanting to stretch in this area, and asked me, as the spontaneous one in the house, to help. You might see where this one is going . . . grin. So I made the random suggestion on a weeknight that we go out for frozen yogurt after dinner—a date—on a work night. He fought me for a while, but he eventually gave in.

After we got back I asked him how he felt. He replied that he was calm, refreshed, energized, and at peace—whereas before we left he had been anxious, tired, and somewhat worried.

This was the result of *one act* of spontaneity. Just one! Imagine if every time you did something spontaneous you got these results? How much more exciting would life be? How much energy would you have for your work, your family, and yourself?

Though spontaneity is supposed to be *spontaneous*, I'm guessing sometimes it can be hard for you to come up with ideas of spontaneous things to do, especially when you're stressed or tired. Here is a list of ideas to get you started. You don't have to memorize them; just let them get you started with your own ideas. Having these things in your mind should help you draw upon them when that urge to be spontaneous pops up!

- ✓ Do a cartwheel (and if you're brave, do it in public)
- ✓ Dance in the rain
- ✓ Go for ice cream on a week night
- ✓ Go to the playground and swing on the swings (see Way 1)
- ✓ Go to a movie on your lunch break
- ✓ Grab some sidewalk chalk and start coloring your driveway
- ✓ Play in the sprinkler
- ✓ Keep Play-Doh at your desk and play with it (see Way 2)
- ✓ Get something that makes noise when you squeeze it or push it. Then squeeze it or push it.
- ✓ Go for a scenic drive for the fun of it

- ✓ Stop by the animal shelter on a whim and visit with the animals

- ✓ Get up and stretch

- ✓ Play with toys—without kids

- ✓ Get out the kids' crayons and color a picture (see Way 17)

I hope this list will get your creative juices flowing. When the next opportunity to be spontaneous arises, latch onto it and ride it to positive results!

WAY 17

Color Your Time

There's nothing quite like the smell of Crayola crayons to bring memories of childhood rushing back through your mind. Memories of coloring books spread across the kitchen table with a pile of colorful crayons to choose from, your kindergarten masterpiece hanging from the fridge, your hands smelling like colored wax for days. These memories can bring a smile to your face.

Coloring is a fun activity I believe adults should still engage in today, but for this Way I want to take it a step further. I discovered this exercise from the book *Write. 10 Days to Overcome Writer's Block. Period.* by Karen Peterson, Ph. D. It is an exercise I have begun to use in one of my workshops. The idea behind it is to create a right-brain time management schedule that helps satisfy your right brain so your left side can produce more. I use this schedule myself to craft my day's activities and have found myself more focused and productive when I stick to it. And I encourage you to check out the book mentioned above if you want a more in-depth explanation of the process and why it works.

Step 1: Print out or draw a blank weekly schedule

Your blank schedule should have the days of the week across the top and hours of the day down the left-hand side. It helps if you have a grid so each time slot gets a block under each day. I use a program like Microsoft Excel and create borders, then print it out for Step 2.

Step 2: Get your coloring utensils ready

If waxy crayons aren't your thing, go for colored pencils. Make sure you have a good assortment of colors. A basic sixteen-pack of crayons or twelve-pack of colored pencils will give you plenty of variety to work with. Try to stick with under twenty colors, as more may get confusing.

Step 3: Empty your mind

This step is crucial for the success of this project. If you begin to analyze anything after this step, your right brain will not be able to complete its task and it will defeat the entire purpose of this exercise.

Step 4: Color with your non-dominant hand

Your non-dominant hand is linked to your right brain. This means your right brain is literally controlling it. Your right brain needs to feel fulfilled. By coloring with the hand "linked" to your right brain, you are opening a rarely used line of communication. The secret to this step is to not think. You may find yourself thinking about what color to choose next, or coloring in your schedule in a pattern that makes sense. Don't. Don't think; let your brain wander. Sometimes it's better to give your left brain something to think about while coloring "mindlessly." Play music and sing along with it. Think about a project you're working on, your family, your next trip to the store—anything besides what you are coloring. Let your hand choose the colors and let it go.

You will probably find your boxes getting colored in a completely unorganized fashion. Instead of going left to right or top to bottom, your hand may skip around. It may also choose colors at random, and then re-choose them later. Let it happen until your entire grid is filled in and colored.

Step 4: Analyze

By now your left brain is probably aching to analyze what your right brain put down on paper. Put down your coloring tools, close your eyes, and breathe deeply three times. When you open your eyes, take a fresh look at your time grid. What colors stand out to you? What do you *feel* when you see different colors?

When I did this exercise, I noticed black was put down for parts of the evenings and mornings I was normally worn out. Yellow was a color I put in the mornings when I first woke up, and it's a color that invokes a feeling of happiness when I look at it. Then I had blocks of red, green, and blue sprinkled throughout.

You will have a similar assortment of colors, but the colors may mean something different to you.

Go with your gut—your feelings—when you analyze what your colors mean.

Step 5: Act!

As much as your daily routine allows, you should try scheduling activities inside your color blocks based on how those activities make you *feel*. It isn't impossible, even if you have a 9–5 day job. If blue makes you feel relaxed, schedule relaxing activities during your blue times. If yellow makes you happy, schedule your favorite things to do during those times.

As you restructure your schedule around what your right brain told you in this exercise, you will find your right brain becoming more satisfied and your left brain more productive and focused! Try your new schedule for a few weeks and note what results you get. Make sure to revisit your right brain schedule every few months, as your colors and activities may change the more you satisfy your right brain's cravings.

WAY 18

ThinkGeek

I couldn't write a book about being a kid again without a chapter on my favorite toy store for grown-ups, ThinkGeek.com (thanks to my business coach Bob Jenkins for getting me hooked on this site). Every time someone new visits my office, they ask about items I got at ThinkGeek. From giant plush microbes (I have Book Worm and Brain Cell) to Smart Mass Thinking Putty (see Way 2), grownup toys are scattered around my office, most within hand's reach for when I get the urge to do something spontaneous and play (see Way 16).

One of the main reasons I love ThinkGeek is the company's (and employees') refusal to grow up. I have finally found a place where adults believe in the power of daily play, being silly, and making life *fun* without restraint. Read some of their website copy to see what I mean.

Speaking of website copy, another reason I love ThinkGeek is their brilliant marketing. If you're in business, take a couple of hours to study their website. Here are a few business lessons I've picked up from the ThinkGeek.com website. I'm sure you'll discover many more:

They make it super easy for customers to find what they're looking for. All their items are grouped by categories, including special interest categories like Star Trek, Dr. Who, and bacon. Whether you're looking for something under $10 for that special geek in your life or a new USB hub for your office, you can find it within a couple of clicks.

Their copy is playful, entertaining, and informative. Every item description makes me laugh. They include a lot of the inside jokes in their copy that geeks, their target audience, will get. One day I took three hours and read their website top to bottom. All their copy was congruent. It all had the same "flavor" and tone. I didn't browse to another page that had a different feel to the writing—it seemed as if the same person wrote all of it. And their copy is hilarious! The entertainment of their copy makes customers want to read more. And customers that read more buy more. Genius.

They stay on top of their industry. Technology is always changing, and the ThinkGeek staff continuously scours the Internet for the latest and greatest items to add to their site. Even if your business is service-based, you can take a lesson from ThinkGeek in the importance of staying up to date with your industry. Know the trends, know what's new, and become *the* go-to expert in your industry.

Creativity is everywhere. Instead of "Shopping Cart," their cart is called "Loot." Instead of stating its status as "Empty," theirs says, "Your cart is lonely." Instead of "Contact Us," their contact page link is "Bug us." And the best part of this strategy for creatively renaming common website links is, they make sense. I've experimented with creative links on my own sites and it's difficult to be creative and clear at the same time. The Geek Overlords (as they call themselves) at ThinkGeek have mastered this creative method.

Their marketing is consistent. Every newsletter has a standard look that matches their website.

In everything they do, overall branding is intact, including fonts, colors, and spacing. Their newsletter hits my inbox consistently. Their Facebook page stays updated. Their Twitter stream spits out announcements on a continuous basis. They're largely successful, not just because they market to a specific niche, but because they make an effort to stay in contact with their niche—where their niche hangs out.

They continuously ask for feedback from their customers and soon-to-be customers. In an act of pure genius, they added the Facebook comments plugin under every item for sale on their site, with a call to action above that says, "Wanna chat about [item name]?" This gets conversations started with their fans, then their fans' friends see the conversation on their Facebook walls, then they go check out what their friends are talking about, and ThinkGeek has almost instantly reached hundreds of new people who had never heard of them before.

Customers are rewarded. Like any good retail outlet, ThinkGeek has a rewards system that gives Geek Points to their customers for every purchase. Those points can then be redeemed for items on the site, with an additional small purchase. This keeps people coming back for more free items *and* spending more money to get those free items, which earns them even more Geek Points to start the cycle all over again. They also run a regular contest of "Customer Action Shots" where customers can upload photos taken of ThinkGeek items in "action" and win prizes. This is another way ThinkGeek shows potential new customers that people aren't only buying their products, but *enjoying* them, too.

I could easily write more about this company. If you run a business, hop on over to ThinkGeek. com today and take a look at what they're doing. Ask yourself how you can apply the ideas above (or other ideas you come up with after viewing the site) to your own business.

If you don't have a business, go to ThinkGeek.com anyway and take a look around. Just keep an eye on the time and don't blame me if you lose an entire day to browsing their site!

Resources in this Way:

 ThinkGeek.com

WAY 19

Action Figures

Admit it, there are some days playing with Barbie or *The Avengers* action figures sounds like amazing fun. Or if you're like me, R2D2 and C3PO wheel their way around your desk every so often. Action figures are some of the best toys ever invented. No other toy allows you to pretend you're someone else, create impossible scenarios, and find even more impossible escapes from those scenarios. From reenacting a scene from your favorite movie to coming up with new scenes with your imagination, action figures allow your inner child to come out and play.

And for adults, action figures can have another stress-reducing effect: role-play. Think about the last time your family got together and things didn't go well. Was someone bothering you? Do you have a nagging mother who only sees your imperfections? Do your siblings not agree with anything you do? Do you feel sometimes the only option to be able to live your own life is to disown your family?

The worst way to handle family dysfunction is to ignore it. Some people bottle their feelings up inside until the point they have a mental breakdown. Then suddenly their friends wonder what happened to them. They seem to snap, when in truth the pressure has been building up for so long it was simply a matter of time before they had to succumb to it. Most of the time the people who seem to have it all together on the outside are the ones falling apart on the inside (see Way 8).

I'd like to suggest a less self-destructive alternative. Next time you find yourself having a conflict with your dysfunctional family (and let's face it, all families are dysfunctional) and wish you could let off some emotional steam, get out your action figures. Take out your frustration on your Borg of a father with your Captain Picard figure. Use Luke Skywalker to blow up the Death Star of a situation and leap in the air with a celebratory, "Whoop! Whoop!" Defeat the "bad guy" through play and release that tension and stress you're holding inside.

Then breathe deeply and confront the problem situation head on calmly and with clarity of thought, with none of the destructive emotions that were once in turmoil inside your gut. You may find the situation resolves itself faster than if you hadn't taken time out to play.

And if you don't have any action figures at home, run to the nearest toy store and grab a couple of your favorite characters (remember the "bad guy" as well). Have fun role-playing your family or other dysfunction and finding peaceful solutions to problematic situations!

WAY 20

Skip Rocks

Imagine for a moment. You're standing at the edge of a lake, its water shimmering with the rising sun. You glance down and see a shiny rock, perfectly shaped for skipping. Reaching down, you pick it up and rub your fingers over its smooth surface. It feels like polished glass. You stretch your arm back, positioning the stone in between your fingers in preparation to flick it out over the water. Then your arm surges forward and you release the rock.

One skip. Two skips. Three skips. Four. Plunk! Each skip sends infinite ripples across the sheer surface. The final "Plunk!" creates a surge of ripples enveloping the previous four and you watch as they interact with each other, reaching far into the surrounding waters. You wonder if those ripples could go on forever, as they seem to fade over time. And you reach down for another stone to begin the process all over again.

Skipping rocks (or shells if you're at the beach) is a relaxing activity that naturally lends itself to contemplation and thought. If you have a decision weighing heavily on your mind, I encourage you to find some water and skip a few rocks. Take time to relax, enjoy nature, and study the ripples your rocks create. Open your mind up to infinite possibilities, just as the ripples become infinite.

Then imagine yourself in the middle of that decision as the rock you're about to throw. What kind of ripples will you send? Will they gently massage the people affected by your decision much like ripples in a lake massage the plants below, releasing oxygen and life-giving nutrients? How far can your life-giving ripples reach? Do you even know? What if they could reach to the edge of the lake, touching everything and everyone in your life—and beyond?

You will never know until you let the rock of your decision soar. So do it. Right now. Take the decision in your hand. Reach back and throw your arm in front of you. Let the decision soar and let your ripples expand to touch the world around you. You never know what effect your ripples will have and whose life will be changed because you chose to act!

WAY 21

Dance

If you read the Dedication in this book, you probably recognized the poem on which it's based. This poem is popular for a reason. Deep inside, we all desire to dance like no one is watching, sing like no one is listening, love like we've never been hurt, and live like there's nothing to fear. But the fact is, no matter how much we repeat this mantra to ourselves, we rarely live up to it.

Why? Why is it so hard to dance like no one is watching? Why is it hard to let go, let loose, and not worry about what others think? Why do we have to protect ourselves behind the barrier of perfectionism? And even worse, what result is this having on our careers, our goals, our relationships—our *lives?*

Perfectionism, fear of what others think, fear of failure, fear of success, it is all based in one root—fear. Fear is not all bad. After all, it's good to be afraid of things that might hurt us, such as poisonous snakes, so we can avoid potentially dangerous situations. But if we live in fear we will accomplish nothing; we will not make an impact in our world; and we will be doomed to live in a constant state of nervousness, frustration, and anxiety.

And as someone who has been to the brink of a life ruled by anxiety and fear, let me be the first to tell you—that is *no way to live!*

So what can we do? How can we act on the poem's advice and begin to *truly live* like there's nothing to fear? The solution is so easy it's mind boggling and scary.

We dance. We sing. We love. And in doing these three things with reckless abandon, without being stopped by what others think about us or our imperfections, we *live*.

I have started playing with this concept at work. When I or members of my team are getting ready to tackle a big project, I put on one of my favorite dancing songs, "All Star" by Smash Mouth, and *literally dance* around the office. Dancing gets your body moving, your blood flowing, your endorphins rising, and your smile shining. And dancing like no one is watching, well, that usually gets the best medicine going as well—laughter.

If you can learn to dance like no one is watching, no matter how silly you may look or how imperfect your dance routine may be, singing like no one is listening and loving like you've never been hurt before will come more naturally to you. Each one is a step toward living like there's nothing to fear. Each step will stretch you a little further. And with each step you will become more confident in your goals, dreams, choices, and relationships.

And at the end of it all, when you're truly living like there's nothing to fear, you *will* change your life. And if all of us can do this together, we can change the *entire* world.

About the Author

Kristen Eckstein, the Ultimate Book Coach, is a sought-after independent publishing expert and award-winning international speaker. Her reputation is to create books that build your business through Ghost Publishing, a term she coined to define her exclusive done-for-you independent publishing program.

Kristen loves books—reading them, writing them and helping other people publish them. She has been interested in all aspects of books ever since she was 5 when she read her first Nancy Drew book. In 2003, Kristen began her book career when she served as the Marketing Director for a vanity publishing company that featured a traditional publishing arm. During this time she learned the ins and outs of vanity, subsidy and traditional publishing—what to look for, what to avoid and how to make sure authors don't get ripped off.

Ultimately, Kristen left that publishing company behind and co-founded Imagine!Studios LLC, an art and media production company, with her husband. They soon began publishing authors' books again under their own label. Relocation caused them to hand that portion of their business off to another capable publisher and Kristen began her role as an independent publishing book coach. In 2011 Kristen founded the "21 Ways" series of pocket guidebooks under the traditional publishing label of her company, Discover! Books.

Now Kristen spends her time helping others get into print. To date she has started 42 publishing companies and published 107 books and eBooks. She has taken a complicated publishing process and broken it down step by step through her Ghost Publishing method which puts the author in control of the process. Do you have a book you've been meaning to write? Let Kristen Eckstein help you publish the book that will bring you business!

Learn more about Kristen at
www.UltimateBookCoach.com

Collect them all!

Look for more *21 Ways*™ books at
21WaysBooks.com

www.ingramcontent.com/pod-product-compliance
Lightning Source LLC
Chambersburg PA
CBHW052103070526
44584CB00017B/2320